Bible Studies for the Life of Excellence

A Study of James

by Bob and Rose Weiner

"Daniel was preferred above the presidents and princes, because an excellent spirit was in him; and the king thought to set him over the whole realm...forasmuch as he was faithful, neither was there any error or fault found in him"

Daniel 6:3-4

Cover Photograph
By
Jerry Sieve

30th Printing
June 2000

Contact for more information:

MARANATHA PUBLICATIONS
P.O. Box 1799
Gainseville, FL 32602
(904) 645-3965
(904) 645-3966 fax

website: http://www.mpi2000.net

Bible Studies
for the
Life of Excellence

Table of Contents

Scripture references in *Bible Studies for the Life of Excellence* are designed for use with the *New American Standard Version Bible*.

"Bob and Rose Weiners' Bible Studies have helped countless thousands of new believers become established on sound biblical truth. We have also found that believers of all ages have benefited greatly from them. Many even go through them once a year to strengthen their foundations. It is understandable that they are now considered a standard for such studies."   *-- Rick Joyner, MorningStar Publications and Ministries*

INTRODUCTION

This epistle was written by James, the brother of Jesus. In the salutation of this epistle James simply refers to himself as a servant of God and of the Lord Jesus Christ. Although James himself was the brother of our Lord it was his glory to serve Jesus in the Spirit rather than boast of being kin to Him in the flesh. At least sixteen times he refers to his readers as *brethren*, recognizing what Jesus had said to him when He and His mother and brothers had come seeking after Him, "Who is My mother, My brother, My sister, those who do the will of God."

James did not begin to believe in Jesus until after His resurrection. His life was ended by martyrdom. The Jews had demanded of James a public denial of belief in Jesus. When James stood upon the balcony in the temple and cried out that Jesus was the Messiah, the Son of the Living God, he was thrown from the battlements of the temple. Since the fall did not kill him, he was beaten to death with a club while he was on his knees praying, "Father forgive them for they know not what they do."

This epistle reveals a life of noble character. It is a book of wisdom, a type of New Testament proverbs, which are like a string of pearls, each being a separate entity in itself. Because of this, the book is nearly impossible to outline. In this study we will try to dig underneath some of the gems of wisdom, comparing scripture with scripture, in an attempt to glean the precious truths that are given there. In short, the book deals with the essence of Christianity—faith, hope, and love—in proverbial form interspersed with exhortations, words of comfort and encouragement, as well as warnings and reproofs.

1. *It is full of faith* - The truths of faith are laid down which basically are this: faith without works is like the body without the spirit—*dead!* James challenges us to action, exhorting us to be a doer of the word and not a hearer only.

2. *It is full of love* - James is full of practical ways in which love can be demonstrated which could be summed up in this passage:

    > *If any one thinks himself to be religious and yet does not bridle his tongue...*
    > *this man's religion is worthless.*
    > *This is pure and undefiled religion in the sight of our God and Father,*
    > *to visit orphans and widows in their distress, and to keep oneself unstained by the world.*
    > *James 1:26-27*

    This book could be called "a book for the tongue" since James' teaching on: bridling the tongue, being a respector of persons, and spiritual adultery, hits right at the core of the two commandments which Jesus gave to the church. He said, "Love the Lord thy God with all thy heart, soul, mind and strength and love thy neighbor as thyself."

3. *It is full of hope* - As we study this epistle we discover what our attitude toward the future should be and the hope that is before us as those living in the last days.

STUDY 1

A GENERAL EPISTLE

1. How are we to react to trials? (James 1:2)
    _____

2. What does the testing of your faith produce? (James 1:3)
    _____

3. As we endure or have patience, we will stand upon the Word without murmuring or complaining. What is the result of having endurance or patience worked into your life? (James 1:4; Luke 21:19; Heb. 6:12)
    a. _____
    b. _____
    c. _____

4. If you lack wisdom, what are you to do and what will be the result? (James 1:5)
    _____

5. What is the condition for asking and receiving? (James 1:6-8)
    _____

6. We see an example of this when Peter was walking on the waters. What did he do that caused him to start sinking? (Matt. 14:29-31)
    _____

    What did Jesus say to him? (Matt. 14:31)
    _____

Peter was rebuked for not simply accepting the Word of God as truth. Many times people get the idea that faith is very abstract. They feel they must strive and strain to believe the Word, confessing it constantly, meditating on it, trying to get enough of that big package of faith to make God's Word come to pass.

Actually this idea is carnal. Faith is much simpler than this. Here is an example:

Jane met Mary at a meeting. After talking together for about an hour they became good friends. They made a luncheon appointment for the next day at noon. The next day they were both there right on time. Notice that Jane did not spend her time being anxious, hoping and trying to believe with all her heart that Mary would show up for lunch according to her word. Jane merely *accepted Mary's word as fact* and was there the next day, expecting Mary to arrive on time.

7. What then, should our attitude be toward God's Word? (I John 5:9)
    _____

Therefore, true faith is not striving, straining and trying to believe, but it is merely accepting God's Word as truth, just (and even more) as we would accept the word of a friend.

8. In James 1:9-10 we see James referring to a parable of Jesus. What lesson do we learn from it? (Luke 14:7-11)
    _____

9. Therefore, instead of feeling inferior or superior to one another,
    a. What should the brother of humble circumstances glory in? (James 1:9)

    _____

    b. What should the brother who is rich glory in? (James 1:10)

    _____

10. What should we all remember? (James 1:11; I Peter 1:24-25)

    _____

11. What is the reward for one who perseveres under trial? (James 1:12)

    _____

12. As we are persevering in a trial, what should be our attitude? (I Peter 3:14-16)
    a. _____
    b. _____
    c. _____
    d. _____
    e. _____

13. During times of testing, what should we remember? (I Peter 4:12-14)
    a. _____
    b. _____
    c. _____

14. When will the crown of life be given—in this world or in the next? (James 1:12)

    _____

15. Who are those that experience these trials? (James 1:12)

    _____

16. Does God test men, and what is the purpose? (Deut. 8:2-5)
    a. _____
    b. _____
    c. _____
        _____
    d. _____

17. Who is the tempter? (James 1:13-14)

    _____

18. If a man yields to temptation, what will happen in his heart and life? (James 1:14-15)
    a. _____
    b. _____
    c. _____

19. Where does every good and perfect gift come from? (James 1:17)

    _____

20. If anyone says they are fellowshipping with God and yet walk in darkness, what are they doing? (I John 1:5-6)

    _____

21. How are we to walk and what provision is there for us? (I John 1:7)
    a. _____
    b. _____
    c. _____

22. What else do we know about God? (James 1:17; Mal. 3:6)
    a. _____
    b. _____
    c. _____

23. How were we born again? (James 1:18)
    a. _____
    b. _____

24. What are we to God? (James 1:18)

    _____

The first fruits were those portions of the fruit of the earth, beast, and man that were sacred to God. These belonged completely to God, being given totally to Him as an offering.

25. Therefore, what is our reasonable service as Christians, and what is the mark of the overcomer? (Rom. 12:1; Rev. 14:1-4)
    a. _____
    b. _____

NOTES

NOTES

STUDY 2

OUR CONVERSATION AND WALK

1. What three things are we exhorted to do as Christians? (James 1:19)
   a. _____
   b. _____
   c. _____

2. When someone does a lot of talking, what is unavoidable? (Prov. 10:19)
   _____

3. What type of person restrains his speaking, and what are his words compared to?
   (Prov. 10:19-20)
   a. _____
   b. _____

4. How can you know the voice of a fool? (Eccl. 5:3)
   _____

5. What then should we do about our speech? (Eccl. 5:2, 6-7)
   a. _____
   b. _____
   c. _____

6. What does the Word say about those who have a quick temper and what they can do
   about it? (Prov. 14:17; 15:1-2; 16:32)
   a. _____
   b. _____
   c. _____
   d. _____
   e. _____

7. When we correct or rebuke someone in wrath, what does it do? (James 1:20)
   _____

8. How are these qualities and fruits of the Spirit developed in our life? (James 1:21)
   a. _____
   b. _____

9. What is the implanted or engrafted Word, and what is it able to do? (James 1:21)
   a. _____
   b. _____

Grafting is the process by which one portion of a plant is made to unite with another plant. An incision is made into the original plant and a branch is inserted. These two are bound together with a cord, and they grow and become one. It is the same with receiving the Word and letting it be engrafted into our soul. As it grows and becomes one with us, our souls shall begin to be transformed.

10. What does Paul call this process? (Eph. 4:23)
    _____

11. What then are we exhorted to be? (James 1:22)

_____

12. What is a hearer and not a doer of the Word likened to? (James 1:23-24)

_____
_____

Read II Peter 1:4-11.

13. How do we partake of the divine nature? (II Peter 1:4)

_____

14. The next few scriptures list some spiritual qualities. If a person lacks these qualities, what has he done? (II Peter 1:9)
    a. _____
    b. _____

We are exhorted throughout the epistle to put on the new creation or new nature. When we come to the Lord, all we know is what we used to be—that is, bound under Satan's power. Many Christians continue to believe, even after salvation, that they are still like they used to be. They are men who look into the mirror of the Word, then go away and forget what they are as a new creation.

15. What does the Word tell us? (II Cor. 5:17)

_____
_____

Many Christians walk in bondage and in many old habits because they read the above scripture, and then go away, forgetting what kind of person they _now_ are.

16. What must we stop doing? (Eph. 4:17-18)
    a. _____
    b. _____

17. What will alienate us from the life of God? (Eph. 4:18)

_____

Therefore, we must be more than a hearer of the Word, we must walk away from the Word believing that what it says about us as a new creation is true. The Word of God is like a mirror reflecting God's glory. As we look into it, we see what we _are_ as new creatures. The Word also examines our hearts and shows us when we are not walking in the manner of the new creation life.

18. How do we become a doer of the Word? (James 1:25)
    a. _____
    b. _____
    c. _____
    d. _____

Being a doer of the Word means _acting_ like what God says is true. If the Word says "God shall supply all your needs" then you _cannot_ walk away and worry about your finances. If the Word says "the love of God is shed abroad in your heart by the Holy Spirit," then you thank God for the love that is in your heart—you do not walk away and pray for more love.

19. According to Jesus, what is the doer of the Word likened unto? (Matt. 7:24)

_____

20. What came against that house and what happened? (Matt. 7:25)
    a. _____
    b. _____

21. What is the one who hears but does not do likened unto? (Matt. 7:26)
    _____

22. What came against that house and what happened? (Matt. 7:27)
    a. _____
    b. _____

23. What is the "Rock" on which we are to build our house? (Matt. 16:15-18)
    _____

24. When we build our house on the Rock of God's revealed Word, what will we receive?
    (Matt. 16:19—Remember, Jesus *is* the Word—II Peter 1:11)
    a. _____
    b. _____
       _____

NOTES

NOTES

STUDY 3

BRIDLING YOUR TONGUE AND LOVING YOUR NEIGHBOR AS YOURSELF

1. As a Christian, what are we exhorted to do? (James 1:26)
   _____

2. What is bridling the tongue? (Psa. 39:1; I Peter 3:10)
   a. _____
   b. _____
   c. _____
   d. _____

3. If you bridle your tongue, what promises will you receive? (I Peter 3:10)
   a. _____
   b. _____

4. What is a good prayer to pray concerning the bridling of your tongue? (Psa. 141:3)
   _____

5. What is pure and undefiled religion in God's sight? (James 1:27)
   a. _____
   b. _____

6. What should be our attitude toward worldly ways? (I John 2:15-16)
   _____

7. What are some of these worldly ways? (I John 2:16)
   a. _____
   b. _____
   c. _____

8. Therefore, if we seek to be a friend to these ways, what are we? (James 4:4)
   a. _____
   b. _____

9. What are we exhorted to do in James 2:1-8?
   _____

10. If we judge men by outward appearance, what have we become? (James 2:4)
   _____

11. If we dishonor a child of God because of their outward appearance, who have we really dishonored? (James 2:5)
   _____

12. What do those who are rich have more of a tendency to do than those who are poor? (James 2:6-7)
   a. _____
   b. _____
   c. _____

13. How can you avoid becoming a respector of persons? (James 2:8)

   _____

14. If you show partiality, then what are you doing and what will happen? (James 2:9)
   a. _____
   b. _____

15. If we offend in this point, then what are we guilty of breaking? (James 2:10-12)

   _____

16. By what law are we judged as a new creation? (James 2:12)

   _____

17. What is the law of liberty? (Matt. 22:36-40)
   a. _____
   b. _____

18. For those who have not shown mercy, how will their judgement be? (James 2:13)

   _____

19. How will we be judged? (Psa. 18:25; Luke 6:38)

   _____
   _____

NOTES

STUDY 4

FAITH AND WORKS

Read James 2:14-26.

1. What makes faith alive and powerful? (James 2:17)

_____

The Amplified Version of the above verse reads:

> *So also, faith, if it does not have works*
> *(deeds and actions of obedience to back it up)*
> *by itself is destitute of power—inoperative and dead.*

2. What was an example of Abraham's works? (James 2:21)

_____

3. What did this *work* of offering up Isaac show? (James 2:23)

Answer from the Amplified:

> *And the scripture was fulfilled that says Abraham believed—*
> *adhered to, trusted in and relied on God.*

a. _____
b. _____
c. _____
d. _____

Therefore, we see that if we have *faith* in God, then we will *act* according to the Word of God. That *action* is called works.

4. What did this *work* of offering up Isaac, according to the Word of God, do for Abraham's faith? (James 2:22)

_____

The Amplified says, "His faith was completed and reached its *supreme* expression."

5. How did Abraham receive or inherit the promises of God? (Heb. 6:12)

_____

The Amplified Version interprets faith here as:

> *The leaning of the entire personality on God in absolute trust and confidence in His power,*
> *wisdom, and goodness, and patience as endurance and waiting.*

We have seen then, that faith means more than believing that the Word is true, but it means acting on the Word received.

6. What characterized Abraham's reaction to God's Word? (Gen. 22:1-3)

_____

7. We see an example of how Abraham's faith was completed or made perfect by the name he gave to the Lord. What is that name and what does it mean? (Gen. 22:14 and margin).

    _____

8. Because of Abraham's work of obedience which showed his faith in God, what blessing did he receive? (Gen. 22:16-18)

    _____

    _____

9. What else did this kind of faith bring to Abraham? (James 2:23)
    a. _____
    b. _____

The Amplified Version reads:

> *And this was accounted to him as righteousness*
> *(as conformity to God's will in **thought** and deed)*
> *and he was called God's friend.*

To be called a friend of God then, we see that we must have the "Faith of Abraham." That is a faith that acts on the Word of God.

10. What are the privileges of a *friend* of God? (John 15:14-16; 15:13; Prov. 17:17)
    a. _____
    b. _____
    c. _____
    d. _____
    e. _____

11. Many people say that they believe the Bible from cover to cover. Will this kind of faith alone justify them before God? (James 2:19, 24)

    _____

12. Give an example of Rahab's works. (James 2:25; Heb. 11:31; Josh. 2:12, 18-19; Josh. 6:23)

    _____

    _____

    _____

    _____

13. What is faith without works the same as? (James 2:26)

    _____

14. What is faith without works as empty and meaningless as? (James 2:14-17)

    _____

    _____

15. If God tells you not to worry, what *work* would you do to show your faith in His Word?

    _____

16. If the Word says there is no condemnation in Jesus, what works would you do to demonstrate your faith in that Word?

    _____

17. Who are those who are with the Lamb when He shall overcome this world's system? (Rev. 17:14)

_____

Those who are with Him have been chosen from among those whom God has called to follow Him, for they are faithful—full of faith. They have that faith that is alive and powerful, showing by their deeds and actions that they believe what God says is true.

18. What are those who are doers of the Word and not hearers only - or those who show forth their faith by their works - entitled to? (Rev. 22:14)
    a. _____
    b. _____

19. What will God do for them? (Rev. 3:10; 2:26-28)
    a. _____
    b. _____
    c. _____
    d. _____

The *morning star* in the scriptures represents *Jesus* Himself. To those who are doers of the Word, the Lord of glory will give to them Himself as a possession and as a reward.

20. Under the Old Covenant, what inheritance did the Lord give to the priests of Israel in the promised land? (Num. 18:20; Deut. 18:2)

_____

If this was the promise under the Old Covenant to the priests, which is but a shadow of things to come, what greater fulfillment shall we see under the New Covenant as we have the privilege of receiving the Lord of life Himself as our portion and our inheritance. To know Him is the most valuable experience in life.

> *To whom will you liken God?*
> *It is He who sits above the vault of the earth,*
> *He it is who reduces rulers to nothing.*
> *To whom will you liken Me?*
> *That I should be his equal, says the Holy One.*
> *Lift up your eyes on high*
> *And see who has created these stars.*
> *The One who leads forth their host by number*
> *He calls them all by name;*
> *Because of the greatness of His might and the*
> *strength of His power,*
> *Not one of them is missing.*
> *Say to the cities of Judah,*
> *"Here is your God!"*
> *Like a shepherd He will tend His flock,*
> *In His arms He will gather the lambs,*
> *And carry them in His bosom;*
> *He will gently lead the nursing ewes.*
> *(Portions of Isaiah 40)*

NOTES

STUDY 5

THE TONGUE

1. What is a perfect man according to James? (James 3:2)

   _____

2. What is this type of man able to do? (James 3:2)

   _____

The Amplified Version defines "bridling" as the ability to control the whole body and to curb the entire nature.

3. What two things is the tongue likened to? (James 3:3-5)

   a. _____
   b. _____

4. What do the bit in the horse's mouth and the rudder of a ship have in common?

   _____

5. What else is the tongue likened to? (James 3:5-6)

   _____

6. What is the tongue called and what is it responsible for? (James 3:6)

Answer from the Amplified:

And the tongue is a fire.
The tongue is a world of wickedness set among our members,
contaminating and depraving the whole body and setting on fire the wheel of birth—
the cycle of man's nature—being itself, ignited by hell (Gehenna).

   a. _____
   b. _____
   c. _____
   d. _____

7. Who or what is responsible for igniting the tongue or inspiring the tongue to speak evil things? (James 3:6)

   _____

Notice this word "hell" means "Gehenna" in the Greek which is the lake of fire of eternal damnation. It stands in this passage for the demonic powers of that realm which inspire this evil use of the tongue.

8. With what fruit shall the innermost part of your being be satisfied? (Prov. 18:20)

   _____

9. What is in the power of the tongue? (Prov. 18:21)

   _____

10. Give an example of two types of speaking and the fruit each one produces. (Prov. 12:18)

    a. _____
    b. _____

11. Describe the tongue of a wise man and its fruit. (Prov. 15:1-4)

a. _____

b. _____

c. _____

12. Describe the tongue of a foolish man and its fruit. (Prov. 15:1-4; 18:6-7)

a. _____

b. _____

c. _____

d. _____

e. _____

f. _____

13. What does Paul exhort us to avoid in our conversation? (Eph. 5:4)

a. _____

b. _____

c. _____

14. To what does Proverbs liken a person who is always jesting or joking? (Prov. 26:18-19)

_____

This verse is describing a man who is throwing fiery darts for Satan. He is a madman because he is aiding Satan in helping him defeat his Christian brother by destroying the person with his words. There are enough mental harassments from the attacks of demonic spirits without our aiding Satan by flinging fire brands and arrows at our brothers and sisters in the Lord. It is *madness,* for we are destroying the very Kingdom of God which we are trying to build.

15. Where there is no one to spread gossip, what ceases? (Prov. 26:20)

_____

16. What is a contentious man who kindles strife likened to? (Prov. 26:21)

a. _____

b. _____

17. When a person is backbiting or passing rumors and you listen, where do his words lodge? (Prov. 26:22)

_____

18. When a person is contentious and causes strife, speaking with mean and cruel words, what is the *root* cause? (Prov. 26:26, 28)

_____

19. If this man *continues* in his bitterness and harsh speaking what will happen to him? (Prov. 26:26-27; Matt. 12:36-37)

a. _____

b. _____

c. _____

d. _____

e. _____

_____

20. According to Jesus, what is the source of the words of the mouth? (Matt. 12:34-35)

_____

21. Can we tame our tongue? (James 3:7-8)

_____

22. Is it possible then, to bring our tongue into subjection to the spirit? (Rom. 7:24-25)

_____

23. The scripture teaches us that it is the root of bitterness and hatred in our hearts that causes us to be full of venom and poison. How can we get rid of this bitterness and hatred? (James 5:16; Matt. 5:44-48; Matt. 18:34-35; Eph. 5:26)

   a. _____

   _____

   b. _____
   c. _____
   d. _____

24. After we have done all this, what attitude of mind and heart are we to have? (Eph. 4:27-32)

   a. (v.27) _____
   b. (v.29) _____
   c. (v.29) _____
   d. (v.29) _____
   e. (v.30) _____
   f. (v.31) _____

   _____

   g. (v.32) _____
   h. (v.32) _____

If any man offends not in word, the same is a *perfect* man and able to bring the whole body under the control of the Spirit. If this type of perfection were not possible, then God would have not exhorted us to live this way. Jesus said, "Be ye perfect, as your Father in heaven is perfect."

NOTES

NOTES

STUDY 6

THE WORDS OF OUR MOUTH AND THE MEDITATIONS OF OUR HEART

1. What is the untamed tongue compared to? (James 3:8-12)
   a. _____
   b. _____
   c. _____
   d. _____
   e. _____

2. What are the words of the Lord like? (Psa. 12:6)
   _____

3. How can we speak these words? (Psa. 119:11)
   _____

4. How do you treasure the Word in your heart? (Prov. 2:1-5)
   a. _____
   b. _____
   c. _____
   d. _____
   e. _____
   f. _____
   g. _____

5. When you do this, what will happen? (Prov. 2:5; 10-12)
   a. _____
   b. _____
   c. _____
   d. _____
   e. _____
   f. _____
   g. _____

As we seek the words of the Lord as hidden treasure, God will allow it to be tried in our life in the furnace of testing until it is refined seven times. Seven is the number of completion. God will allow the word to be tried in our lives completely and then it will become a part of us forever.

6. As we speak the pure word or *law* of the Lord, what will it do for men? (Psa. 19:7-8, 11)
   a. _____
   b. _____
   c. _____
   d. _____
   e. _____

7. We have learned that in order to be kept from speaking with wickedness, we have to seek the word of the Lord as hidden treasure. What does Jesus compare the Kingdom of heaven to ? (Matt. 13:44-46)
   a. _____
   b. _____

From this we see that to find hidden treasure or to hunt for pearls, you have to *search* and *dig deep*. Sometimes you have to dig deep in *many* places before you find it. In the parable above, Jesus gives us a principle for digging deep into the Word and finding treasure hidden there.

8. The whole Bible, Old and New Testaments, is full of parables. What does Jesus say is found in these parables? (Matt. 13:34-35)
_____

9. Why is the Bible written in parables and to whom will the parables be explained? (Matt. 13:10-11)
_____
_____

10. Who will explain these parables to us? (Matt. 13:36)
_____

11. The disciples have come to Jesus asking for an explanation of the parable of the tares of the field. Read the parable and the interpretation. (Matt. 13:24-30, 36-43) As we look upon this story in the natural (taking it literally), it appears to be the story of a wealthy farmer who had an enemy who was out to destroy his crops. It seems to have very little to do with us. However, as this parable is given a spiritual application, it takes on great meaning. What is the principle of interpretation here? (I Cor. 15:46)
_____
_____

12. Give the spiritual application for each natural thing written below. (Matt. 13:38-43)
   a. the field _____
   b. the good seed _____
   c. the tares _____
   d. the barn _____
   e. the enemy _____
   f. the harvest _____
   g. the reapers _____
   h. the fire _____

13. Use this principle of interpretation to find the spiritual application behind the conflict between Israel and Assyria in the following passage. (Isa. 10:24-27)
   a. people dwelling in Zion _____
   b. the Assyrian _____
   c. rod and staff of Egypt _____
   d. the yoke _____
   e. the fatness or the anointing _____

(Note: Doing word studies on these words, using the Bible as a dictionary, we find the following definitions—
   1. *Zion* represents the *church*.
   2. Those who *oppose* Zion or Israel, in this case, *Assyria,* always represents the *enemy*, Satan.
   3. *Rod* in the scriptures signifies *authority* while *staff* signifies *guidance*.
   4. *Egypt* always represents the *world* and its *system*.
   5. The *yoke* is that satanic bondage which Jesus came to break. *Fatness* or *the anointing*, as some translations read, signifies the *power of the Holy Spirit* as well as being fat, having fed upon the Spirit revealed Word.)

14. Interpret Isaiah 14:24-27 in light of this principle. What is God's plan for the whole earth?

_____
_____

15. Interpret Isaiah 24:21-23 by comparing it with Revelation 17:12-14.
    a. 1. Host of heaven and the kings of the earth _____
       2. Interpretation _____
    b. Compare Isaiah 24:23 with Revelation 21:23 and Revelation 22:5
       _____

16. Interpret Isaiah 27:1 and 31:8-9.
    a. Leviathan   (Rev. 12:9) _____
    b. Mighty sword   (Eph. 6:17) _____
    c. Standard   (Isa. 30:31) _____
    d. Fire   (Jer. 23:29) _____
    e. Furnace   (Psa. 12:6) _____
    f. Jerusalem and Zion   (Psa. 125:2) _____
       Interpretation _____
       _____
       _____
       _____
       _____
       _____

And they overcame him by the blood of the Lamb,
and the word of their testimony,
and they did not love their life even unto death.
Rev. 12:11

17. Interpret Isaiah 30:25-26.
    a. Moon   (Song of Solomon 6:10) _____
    b. Sun   (Psa. 84:11; Matt. 17:2) _____
    (Note: If the *sun* in the scripture signifies *Jesus,* then the *moon* signifies the *church*, for the church like the moon has no light in itself except the light that it reflects from Jesus, the *Sun* of righteousness.

    Part of the glory, light, and beauty of the natural moon is hidden when the earth casts its shadow upon it in varying degrees, hence the moon waxes and wanes and it is only seen in its full glory and radiance at one time during each month. So also the church is kept from reflecting the full glory, light and brilliance of Jesus, the *Sun*, when the shadow of worldliness and earthly ways can be seen operating it. The church in its history has waxed and waned and even gone into a complete eclipse. However, when the shadows of worldliness are cast aside, then the church can be seen in all its perfection and brilliance, reflecting the pure light of God Himself. God has placed the moon in the sky as a faithful witness to His bride the church. Twelve times a year the witness goes forth, the number twelve telling us that God's divine government will be established. For though the church has waxed and waned because of the darkness of this earth, in the last days, at the end of time, the earth will be unable to cast its shadow upon it to mar or hide its glory and brilliance. For the church will stand as a bright and glorious light in the midst of a crooked and perverse generation.

The heavens are telling of the glory of God;
And their expanse is declaring the work of His hands.
Day to day pours forth speech,
And night to night reveals knowledge.
There is no speech, nor are there words;
Their voice is not heard.
Their line has gone out through all the earth,
And their utterances to the end of the world.
Psalms 19:1-4

c. Seven times brighter   (Lev. 8:33) _____

d. Seven days   (Gen. 2:2) _____

Interpretation _____

_____

_____

_____

_____

_____

_____

(Note: According to Isaiah's prophecy, the moon or church is no longer a mere reflector of the light of the sun, but has become transformed into its *very* image.)

But we all, with unveiled face, beholding as in a mirror the glory of the Lord,
are being transformed into the same image
from glory to glory just as from the Lord, the Spirit.
II Cor. 3:18

And He is the radiance of His glory and the exact representation of His nature
Heb. 1:3

He is the sole expression of the glory of God—
the Light being, the outraying of the divine—
and He is the perfect imprint and very image of God's nature.
Heb. 1:3, Amplified Version

And the glory which Thou hast given me,
I have given to them; that they might be one...
John 17:22

18. What is one way the Assyrian will be terrified and punished? What is the "blow of the rod of punishment" the Lord will lay on him? (Isa. 30:31-32)

_____

These are just a few of the glorious parables in Isaiah. As we search through the Word for hidden treasure and dig deep into it, we will find many pearls of *great price* which will enrich our hearts in the ways of the Lord.

19. As we fill our minds and hearts with the words of God, what will be our condition? (Prov. 3:13)

_____

20. What are the treasures of wisdom worth to us? (Prov. 3:14-18)
    a. _____
    b. _____
    c. _____
    d. _____
    e. _____

21. As we treasure these things in our heart, what will our conversation be like? (Prov. 25:11-13)
    a. _____
    b. _____
    c. _____

[Remember, *gold* stands for the *pure* or *divine nature* and *silver* for *redeemed man*]. "A word spoken in right circumstances is like the pure and divine nature of God flowing out of redeemed man."

NOTES

NOTES

STUDY 7

GODLY WISDOM, WORLDLY FRIENDSHIP AND OUR ATTITUDE TOWARD SINNERS

1. How is a man of wisdom and understanding to act? (James 3:13)

   _____

2. Describe the wisdom of this world. (James 3:14-15)
   a. _____
   b. _____
   c. _____
   d. _____
   e. _____

3. What is the source of this wisdom? (James 3:15)

   _____

4. What does jealousy and selfish ambition produce? (James 3:16)
   a. _____
   b. _____

5. Describe the wisdom of God from above. (James 3:17)
   a. _____
   b. _____
   c. _____
   d. _____
   e. _____
   f. _____
   g. _____
   h. _____

6. What is the fruit of seed sown in this manner? (James 3:18)

   _____

[This word "Righteousness" means conformity to God's will in thought and deed.]

7. Who else was a peacemaker and what did he do? (Gen. 13:7-9)

   _____

8. What is the source of quarrels and conflicts? (James 4:1-2)
   a. _____
   b. _____

9. What great sin did James accuse them of committing and what did he mean by this? (James 4:2; I John 3:15)

   _____

10. Why do you not have what you need or want? (James 4:2, John 16:24)

   _____

11. What is the reason why some don't receive? (James 4:3)

   _____

12. What is spiritual adultery? (James 4:4)

_____

13. What is friendship with the world? (I John 2:15-16)
   a. _____
   b. _____
   c. _____
   d. _____

So we see, to commit adultery with the world, we have to go against the teachings of God and walk after the ways of the world.

14. How does friendship with the world affect your relationship with God? (James 4:4)
   a. _____
   b. _____

15. What is to be our attitude toward sinners in the world? (Luke 15:1-2; Rom. 5:8)
   a. _____
   b. _____
   c. _____
   d. _____

16. What are the three parables Jesus gives about sinners and His attitude toward them?

   A.   Luke 15:4-7 _____

         His attitude: a. (v.4) _____
                        b. (v.5) _____
                        c. (v.6) _____
                        d. (v.7) _____

(Jesus always spoke of the Pharisees as those righteous persons who were righteous in their own eyes and didn't see that they needed to repent.)

One who repents is defined in the Amplified Version as one who changes his mind, abhoring his errors and misdeeds, and determines to enter upon a better course of life.

1. Where does Jesus place the lost lamb? (Luke 15:5)

_____

2. We know that Jesus is the *Head* of the Church and we are His body. What part of the body is responsible for His sheep? (Isa. 9:6)

_____

3. We know that Jesus is our High Priest. In the account of the High Priest's garments (who is the type and shadow of Jesus), what does He bear on His shoulders? (Ex. 28:11-12)

_____

   B.   Luke 15:8-10 _____
         His attitude: a. (v.8) _____
                        b. (v.8) _____
                        c. (v.9) _____
                        d. (v.10) _____

1. What is the lamp of Jesus lights in order to seek for the lost coin? (Matt. 5:14-16)

_____

C. Luke 15:11-32 _____

His attitude: a. (v.20) _____
b. (v.20) _____
c. (v.20) _____
d. (v.22) _____
e. (v.23) _____
f. (v.24) _____

1. What type of person (Christian) was the older son? (Luke 15:29)

_____

2. What was his attitude? (Luke 15:28-30)

_____

We must be careful not to be like the older brother in our attitude when a prodigal son comes home and the Father *honors* him.

3. What two blessings did the older son forget to count? (Luke 15:31)
a. _____
b. _____

Many people are like the older son and want all the blessings for themselves. They are jealous and petty in their hearts. They cannot rejoice over the honor of blessings others receive, especially those who have just come into the Kingdom or are younger in the Lord than they are. "It isn't fair," they reason. Yet is God unfair? They have forgotten the *better* part which is the love relationship with the Father.

My child, you have always been with me, and all that is mine is yours.

17. We see this picture of fallen man and his restoration in Daniel in the picture of Nebuchadnezzar. In relating Nebuchadnezzar to fallen man as a whole, when shall the Kingdom which Adam lost be restored to man? (Dan. 4:25-26)

_____

18. What happened to Nebuchadnezzar that will happen to fallen man in the last days? (Dan. 4:34)
a. _____
b. _____
c. _____

19. What is his attitude toward the ways of the world? (Dan. 4:35)

_____

20. At this time, when he turned to God with all his heart, praised and honored Him, and turned away from the world, what did he receive? (Dan. 4:36)
a. _____
b. _____
c. _____
d. _____
e. _____

21. What is the attitude and motive of this repentant heart? (Dan. 4:37)

_____

_____

NOTES

STUDY 8

GOD' LOVE, OUR HUMILITY, AND THE DEVIL'S PERSECUTION

1. What is the attitude of God's Spirit toward us? (James 4:5) [The marginal note in the New American Standard Version is "The Spirit which He has made to dwell in us jealously desires us."

   _____

2. Under the Old Covenant, the Spirit of God dwelt in the Holy of Holies in the temple in Jerusalem. What did Jesus' enemies accuse Him of saying? (Matt. 26:61; 27:40)

   _____
   _____

3. What actually happened? (Matt. 27:50-51)

   _____
   _____

After the Spirit of God departed from the temple in Jerusalem, it was not different than any other building. The temple at Jerusalem was destroyed as far as God was concerned.

4. Where is temple of God now? (John 20:20-23; I Cor. 6:17-20)

   _____

5. What other things do we learn from these scriptures?
   a. (John 20:23) _____
   b. (I Cor. 6:17) _____

When God's Spirit comes to dwell in man's spirit the two become intermingled and cannot be separated.

6. Who is God opposed to? (James 4:6)

   _____

7. What should our attitude toward one another be, and who shall be considered the greatest? (Matt. 23:5-12)
   a. (23:8) _____
   b. (23:11) _____

8. What are we exhorted to clothe ourselves with in our attitudes toward one another? (I Pet. 5:5-6)

   _____

9. What two things are we exhorted to do in each of the following passages? (James 4:7; I Pet. 5:6-9)
   a. (4:7) _____
   b. (5:6-9) _____

10. Why are humbling yourself and resisting the devil closely related? (Prov. 16:18)

    _____

11. What is the fear of the Lord? (Prov. 8:13)
    a. _____
    b. _____
    c. _____
    d. _____

12. What attitude of mind are we to have? (I Peter 5:8; 1:13)
    a. _____
    b. _____
    c. _____
    d. _____

13. Where and how is much of our battle fought? (II Cor. 10:3-5)
    a. _____
    b. _____
    c. _____
    d. _____

14. As we submit to God and resist the devil, what will happen? (James 4:7)
    _____

15. As we submit to God and resist the devil, what are we to remember? (I Peter 5:9)
    _____

16. What is one way to give the devil an opportunity? (Eph. 4:26-27)
    _____

17. The early church was full of power, signs and miracles, yet they were not free from persecution, tribulation or attacks from the enemy. What exhortation was given to them? (Acts 14:22)
    a. _____
    b. _____
    c. _____

18. As we resist the devil, firm in the faith, we are not do despair but to remember the same experience of sufferings are being accomplished by the brethren who are in the world. Give examples of this in the following scriptures:
    a. The life of Paul (Acts 9:16; I Thes. 3:1-5) _____
    b. The life of John (Rev. 1:9) _____
    c. The life of Jesus (John 15:18-21) _____
    d. Our life (John 16:33; II Tim. 3:12) _____

19. We are exhorted to follow the example of Christ's suffering, therefore, what should be our reaction to each of the following? (I Pet. 2:21-23)
    a. When reviled _____
    b. When suffering _____
    c. When persecuted (Matt. 5:44) _____

20. As we endure these things, what will be the reward? (II Tim. 2:10-12)
    _____

THE DILIGENT SEEKER, THE REPENTANT HEART, THE RIGHTEOUS JUDGMENT

1. If *we* draw near to God, how will he respond? (James 4:8)

    _____

2. If we seek God, what will He allow us to do? (II Chron. 15:2)

    _____

3. When we draw near to God, what are the two things that we must believe? (Heb. 11:6)
    a. _____
    b. _____

    The Amplified Bible says that "He is the Rewarder of those who *earnestly* and *diligently* seek Him out."

4. As a *diligent* seeker, what are the conditions for receiving from God? (Matt. 7:7)

    Answer from the Amplified:

    > *Keep on asking and it will be given you,*
    > *keep on seeking and you will find,*
    > *keep on knocking (reverently) and the door will be opened to you.*

    a. _____
    b. _____
    c. _____

5. As we seed God diligently in this manner, what will happen? (Matt. 7:8)

    Answer from the Amplified:

    > *For everyone who keeps on asking receives,*
    > *and he who keeps on seeking finds,*
    > *and to him who keeps on knocking it will be opened.*

    a. _____
    b. _____
    c. _____

6. What will this diligent man find? (Col 2:2-3)
    a. _____
    b. _____
    c. _____

7. As we draw near to God, what assurance do we have that He will draw near to us? (James 4:8)

    _____

8. James, Chapter Four has been speaking to those people in the church who have been involved in spiritual adultery—getting involved with friendship with the world and its ways, exalting their opinions above God's Word. What exhortation is given to those who are putting other things above God? (James 4:8)
   a. _____
   b. _____

9. What does James call this type of person? (James 4:8)
   _____

   If we find ourselves being double-minded it might do us well to search our hearts and see if we are putting anything before the Lord.

10. What are we to wash from our hearts? (Jer. 4:14)
    _____

11. How are we to make ourselves clean? (Isa. 16-17)
    a. _____
    b. _____
    c. _____
    d. _____
    e. _____
    f. _____

12. What is the reward for the obedient and for the disobedient? (Isa. 1:19-20)
    a. _____
    b. _____

13. Describe a repentant heart. (James 4:9-10)
    a. _____
    b. _____
    c. _____
    d. _____

14. What exhortation are we given about backbiting? (James 4:11)
    a. _____
    b. _____
    c. _____

15. What *law* are we judging and breaking? (James 2:8)
    _____

There are only *two* laws Jesus gave us to keep under the New Covenant. Woe unto us if we break this one.

16. What is one thing that is an abomination to God? (Prov. 6:16-19)
    _____

17. Who is the only Lawgiver and Judge? (James 4:12)
    _____

18. We are exhorted here not to judge one another in a *backbiting* manner. Yet what does Paul exhort us to do? (I Cor. 6:1-3)

_____

19. What kind of judgment are we exhorted by Jesus to give? (John 7:24)
    a. _____
    b. _____

20. What example do we see of righteous judgment, and who is able to make a righteous judgment? (John 5:30; 8:15-16)
    a. _____
    b. _____
    c. _____
    d. _____
    e. _____

21. What is the difference between a backbiting judgment and a righteous judgment? (I Sam. 16:7)

_____
_____

22. When Moses chose men who were to help judge the tribes of Israel, what were three characteristics that they had to have? (Ex. 18:21)
    a. _____
    b. _____
    c. _____

NOTES

NOTES

STUDY 10

OUR ATTITUDE TOWARD THE FUTURE

1. What should be our attitude toward plans for the future? (James 4:13-15)

    _____

    _____

2. Why should we have this attitude? (James 4:14)

    _____

3. What does Jesus exhort us to be on guard against? (Luke 12:15)

    _____

4. What principle does Jesus put forth in the parable of the rich fool? (Luke 12:16-21)

    _____

    _____

5. For this reason, what attitude does Jesus exhort us to have? (Luke 12:22)

    _____

6. What examples did Jesus give us to look to as examples of trust? (Luke 12:24-28)
    a. _____
    b. _____
    c. _____

7. What does Jesus compare the vanity of anxiety to and what exhortation does He give?
    (Luke 12:25-26)
    a. _____

        _____
    b. _____

        _____

8. What does Jesus say about the value of man to God and God's ability to provide for
    man? (Luke 12:24, 28)

    _____

    _____

   The Bible teaches us that the trees, the sky, the birds, and the flowers were all made for man to
enjoy. If God is so concerned about every living thing to provide for their every need, *how much
more concerned* and *more* able is God to take care of and provide for the *man* whom He created to
have fellowship with Him?

9. What three things does Jesus exhort us not to do? (Luke 12:29)
    a. _____
    b. _____
    c. _____

10. What characterizes the nations of the world? (Luke 12:30)

    _____

11. What does God know, what are we to seek, and what will be the results? (Luke12:30-31)

   a. _____

   b. _____

   c. _____

12. What is God's desire? (Luke 12:32)

   _____

13. What has God given to the one who is good in His sight? (Eccl. 2:26)

   _____

14. What task has God given the sinners and for what purpose? (Eccl. 2:26)

   a. _____

   b. _____

The purpose of creation was to prepare a home for the man God would create. God created man to be the sole object of His love and affection, one with whom He could share His life, His love, His hopes, plans and dreams. Very few men on the face of the earth seek Him. They seek temporal things rather than the God who created man to be His companion. As we give God the companionship and friendship He desires, He is more than willing to provide for our every need. The things of this world are necessary, but they are not the essence of life—they are the by-product. As we seek God and His Kingdom, all these things will be added. If all men everywhere turned their eyes from running to and fro and seeking the things of this earth to seeking the true and living God, He would provide for all.

15. What is the fate of those who trust in and seek riches? (James 5:1-6)

   a. _____

   b. _____

NOTES

STUDY 11

LIVING IN THE LAST DAYS AND PATIENT ENDURANCE

1. What is the Lord waiting for? (James 5:7)

    _____
    _____

We see that the Lord of the harvest is patiently waiting until the produce of His harvest (which is the saints), shall have received the early and late rains. Now *rain* in the scripture refers to the outpouring of the Holy Spirit. In Joel, we find a teaching given by this prophet of the early and late rains which James was refering to.

2. Joel predicts a great period of desolation for the church followed by a great period of restoration. It is this outpouring of the early and latter rains that bring about that restoration. Give a grief description of that restoration that the Lord of the harvest is waiting for. (Joel 2:23-27) [Note: The following words and thier biblical significance- *grain or corn*: the Word of God; *new wine*: joy of the Holy Spirit; *oil*: the anointing of the Holy Spirit].

    _____
    _____
    _____
    _____
    _____
    _____
    _____
    _____

3. What will happen after the outpouring of the early and latter rains which will bring about the restoration of the Church? (Joel 2:28-29)

    _____
    _____

What we have seen is but a first fruit compared to the glory, restoration, and anointing that shall be poured out in the earth.

4. What are we exhorted to do in light of the coming of the Lord? (James 5:8)
    a. _____
    b. _____

5. What did Jesus tell us about standing and being patient in the midst of persecution? (Luke 21:16-19; Matt. 10:22)
    a. _____
    b. _____

6. What did James say about the coming of the Lord? (James 5:8)

    _____

7. In light of this, what word of exhortation does James give? (James 5:9)

    _____
    _____

8. As those living in the last days, what should we be sure to do? (Rom. 13:10-14)
    a. _____
    b. _____
    c. _____
    d. _____
    e. _____

9. What does Peter say about the day in which he lived and what our attitude should be?
    (I Peter 4:7-8)
    a. _____
    b. _____
       _____
    c. _____

We can see from the scriptures that the apostles considered the day in which they were living the last days. According to the scriptures, the last days of time began after the resurrection of the Messiah Jesus. Unfortunately many theologians interpret the last days as the last few years of time, anywhere from a seven year period to a forty year period. However, since the resurrection of Jesus, God began to consummate His plan for the ages. Many things interpreted for the last years of time have already been fulfilled, other things wait for fulfillment. Bible prophecy must therefore be interpreted in light of church history. Remember, Jesus said one day is a thousand years. However, we can conclude that after almost 2,000 years of the last days, while the husbandman has been patient, waiting for the precious produce of the soil, we are in the time of the latter rains.

10. In the same portion of scripture in which the early believers are exhorted about the coming of the Lord, whose example are they exhorted to follow? (James 5:10)
    _____

Noah prophesied for 100 years before the rains and flood came. Abraham waited twenty-five years from the time he received the promise of a son until the time Isaac was born to him.

11. What promise did the patriarchs receive and what example of patience did they leave for us? (Heb. 11:8-10, 13-14)
    a. _____
    b. _____
    c. _____
    d. _____

12. What example of suffering did the prophets leave for us, how did they gain approval, and did they receive that which they prophesied about? (Heb. 11:37-40)
    a. (v. 37) _____
    b. (v. 37) _____
    c. (v. 37) _____
    d. (v. 38) _____
    e. (v. 39) _____
    f. (v. 39) _____

The early Christians and those who followed after them also had this same treatment—they were imprisoned, crucified, thrown to the lions, and dragged behind horeses until their brains were dashed out on the ground. During the Protestant Reformation they were burned at the stake, buried alive, and slaughtered. These all died in faith, not having obtained the promise of His coming, God desiring that without us they should not be made perfect.

13. Who is counted blessed? (James 5:11)

_____

14. What saint's example does James give as an example of endurance and what was the outcome of it? (James 5:11; Job 42:10-17)
    a. _____
    b. _____
    c. _____
    d. _____
    e. _____
       _____
    f. _____
       _____
    g. _____
       _____
    h. _____

We must keep in mind that examples of the prophets were examples set by men who were *not* born again and *not* baptized in the Holy Spirit. They did not know the joy of Jesus living in their hearts. They prophesied *only* as the Holy Spirit *moved upon* them. How much greater testimony and example should we set before the world as those who have the *Shekinah* Glory of God, the presence of the Spirit of His Son, dwelling in our hearts.

15. Since we are surrounded by such a great cloud of witnesses (all those men of faith who have suffered for the gospel), who endured to the end, what are we exhorted to do? (Heb. 12:1-2)
    a. (v. 1) _____
    b. (v. 1) _____
    c. (v. 2) _____

16. If we are tempted to grow weary and lose heart, what are we exhorted to remember? (Heb. 12:3-4)
    a. _____
       _____
    b. _____
       _____

NOTES

NOTES

STUDY 12

CONCLUSION

1. What exhortation are we given in regard to our speech? (James 5:12)
   _____

We as Christians should be known for the truth which we speak. Therefore, we do not have to defend our word or try to convince someone of the truth of our statements.

2. What example did Jesus set for us in regard to this teaching? (Matt. 27:11-14; Isa. 53:7)
   _____

3. What are the following people to do? (James 5:13)
   a. Suffering _____
   b. Cheerful _____

4. What promise do we have from the Lord when we pray in times of suffering? (Psa. 50:15)
   _____
   _____

5. As we let the Word of Christ richly dwell within us, what will spring up within our hearts? (Col. 3:16)
   _____

6. What are the sick to do? (James 5:14)
   _____
   _____

7. What will happen? (James 5:15)
   a. _____
   b. _____
   c. _____

8. What does James suggest as a possible cause of sickness? (James 5:15)
   _____

9. Therefore, what are we encouraged to do in order to receive physical as well as spiritual healing? (James 5:16)
   _____

10. What example do we see of this in the early church? (Acts 19:17-18)
    _____
    _____

11. As the Spirit of the Lord rests upon us, what type of healing and ministry should we be able to bring? (Isa. 61:1-3)
    a. _____
    b. _____
    c. _____
    d. _____
    e. _____
    f. _____
    g. _____

12. What does the effective prayer of a righteous man accomplish, and what is an example? (James 5:16-18)

_____

_____

_____

Whose example are we to follow? (I Peter 2:21)

_____

Notice the Elijah was an Old Covenant man. He was not born again and did not know the joy of the Holy Spirit dwellin within. How much more effective should our prayers be who are members of the new creation of God, filled with the Holy Spirit and power.

13. Give another example of the effective prayer of a righteous man. (Gen. 18:23-32)

_____

14. What type of man does God hear? (John 9:31)
    a. _____
    b. _____

15. If we are God-fearing and do God's will, what will we be assured of? (John 9:31)

_____

16. Therefore, what are we exhorted to do? (Phil 4:6)
    a. _____
    b. _____

17. What will happen? (Phil 4:7)

_____

18. If you turn a backslider from the error of his ways, what will happen? (James 5:19-20)

_____

_____

19. If your brother sins, what are you to do according to the teaching of Jesus? (Matt. 18:15-17)
    a. _____
    b. _____
    c. _____
    d. _____

20. When we go to someone to reprove them, what attitude should we have? (Gal. 6:1)
    a. _____
    b. _____

ANSWERS

*Who is like the wise man and who
knows the interpretation of a matter?
A man's wisdom illumines him and
causes his stern face to beam.
Ecclesiastes 8:1*

STUDY 1

A GENERAL EPISTLE

Correct Answers

1. Consider them all joy.
2. Endurance.
3. a. You will be perfect and complete, lacking in nothing.
   b. By perseverance you will win your souls.
   c. You will inherit the promises.
4. Ask of God and it will be given to you.
5. Ask in faith without doubting.
6. Doubt. "O you of little faith."
7. If we receive the witness of men, the witness of God is greater.
8. Humble ourselves instead of trying to receive honor.
9. a. His high position (in Christ).
   b. His humiliation.
10. The glory of men will pass away, but the Word of the Lord abides forever.
11. The crown of life.
12. a. Do not fear their intimidation.
    b. Do not be troubled.
    c. Sanctify Christ as Lord in your heart.
    d. Be ready to make a defense to every one who asks (in gentleness).
    e. Keep a good conscience.
13. a. Do not be surprised at the fiery ordeal.
    b. To the degree that you share the sufferings of Christ, keep on rejoicing.
    c. The Spirit of glory and of God rests upon you.
14. In this world.
15. Those who love the Lord.
16. a. Yes. To know what is in your heart.
    b. To see whether you will keep His commandments or not.
    c. That you might understand that man lives by everything that proceeds out of the mouth of the Lord.
    d. He disciplines us.
17. Your own evil desires or lust.
18. a. He is enticed by his own lust.
    b. Lust gives birth to sin.
    c. Sin brings forth death.
19. The Father.
20. They are lying and not practicing the truth.
21. a. We are to walk in the light as He is in the light.
    b. We are to have fellowship with one another.
    c. The blood of Jesus cleanses us from all sin.
22. a. Every good thing and every perfect gift is from above.
    b. With Him there is no variation.
    c. He does not change.
23. a. By His will.
    b. By the word of truth.
24. First fruits.
25. a. Present your bodies a living and holy sacrifice.
    b. They are first fruits to God.

OUR CONVERSATION AND WALK

Correct Answers

1. a. Be quick to hear.
   b. Be slow to speak.
   c. Be slow to anger.
2. Transgression.
3. a. A wise person.
   b. Choice silver.
4. Through many words.
5. a. Do not be hasty in word.
   b. Let your words be few.
   c. Do not let your speech cause you to sin.
6. a. A quick-tempered man acts foolishly.
   b. A gentle answer turns away wrath.
   c. A harsh word stirs up anger.
   d. The mouth of fools spouts folly.
   e. He who is slow to anger is better than the mighty, and he who rules his spirit, than he who captures a city.
7. It does not achieve the righteousness of God.
8. a. Put aside all filthiness and wickedness.
   b. Receive the Word implanted in humility.
9. a. The proportion of the Word that has become a part of you.
   b. It is able to save your soul.
10. Being renewed in the spirit of your mind.
11. Doers of the Word.
12. A man who looks into a mirror and goes away, forgetting what kind of person he is.
13. Through the promises in the Word.
14. a. He is blind or shortsighted.
    b. He has forgotten his purification from his former sins.
15. If any man is in Christ he is a new creature; the old things passed away; new things have come.
16. a. Walk no longer in the futility of your mind.
    b. No longer be darkened in your understanding.
17. Ignorance of the Word.
18. a. Look intently at it.
    b. Abide by it.
    c. Do not become a forgetful hearer.
    d. Be an effectual doer.
19. A wise man who built his house upon the rock.
20. a. A storm burst against the house.
    b. It did not fall.
21. A foolish man who built his house upon the sand.
22. a. A storm burst against the house.
    b. It fell, and great was its fall.
23. The revelation knowledge of Jesus.
24. a. The keys of the kingdom of heaven.
    b. Entrance into the eternal kingdom of our Lord and Savior Jesus Christ.

STUDY 3

BRIDLING YOUR TONGUE AND LOVING YOUR NEIGHBOR AS YOURSELF

Correct Answers

1. Bridle our tongue.
2. a. Guarding your ways, that you may not sin with your tongue.
   b. Guarding your mouth as with a muzzle.
   c. Refraining your tongue from evil.
   d. Refraining your lips from speaking guile.
3. a. You will love life.
   b. You will see good days.
4. Set a guard over my mouth; keep watch over the door of my lips.
5. a. To visit orphans and widows in their distress.
   b. To keep oneself unstained by the world.
6. We must not love the world.
7. a. The lust of the flesh.
   b. The lust of the eyes.
   c. The boastful pride of life.
8. a. Guilty of spiritual adultery.
   b. An enemy of God.
9. Not to be a respector of persons or show partiality.
10. Judges with evil motives.
11. God.
12. a. Oppress you.
    b. Drag you into court.
    c. Blaspheme the fair name of Jesus.
13. Love your neighbor as yourself.
14. a. Committing sin.
    b. Convicted by the law as transgressors.
15. The whole law.
16. The law of liberty.
17. a. Love the Lord with all your heart, soul and mind.
    b. Love your neighbor as yourself.
18. Merciless.
19. Whatever measure you deal out to others, it will be dealt to you in return.

STUDY 4

FAITH AND WORKS

Correct Answers

1. Works.
2. He offered up Isaac on the altar.
3. a. Abraham believed God.
   b. He adhered to God.
   c. He trusted in God.
   d. He relied on God.
4. It perfected his faith.
5. Through faith and patience.
6. He was doing God's Word.
7. YHWH-jireh—"The Lord will provide."
8. God would multiply his seed as the stars of the heavens, and as the sand which is on the seashore; his seed would possess the gate of their enemies.
9. a. Righteousness.
   b. He was the friend of God.
10. a. You will know the Father's plans.
    b. You will bear fruit.
    c. Your fruit will remain.
    d. Whatever you ask of the Father, He will give it to you.
    e. God will love you at all times.
11. No.
12. She protected God's servants. She believed what they said and did what she was told to do by tying the scarlet thread in the window.
13. It is the same as the body without the spirit.
14. Not giving to those who have a need, but wishing them well with empty words.
15. Trust the Lord.
16. Resist condemnation and believe that you are justified.
17. The called and chosen and faithful.
18. a. They may have the right to the tree of life.
    b. They may enter by the gates into the city.
19. a. Keep them from the hour of testing.
    b. Give them authority over the nations.
    c. Shall rule them with a rod of iron.
    d. Will give them the morning star.
20. The Lord God Himself was their portion and their inheritance.

STUDY 5

THE TONGUE

Correct Answers

1. One who does not stumble in what he says.
2. Able to bridle the whole body as well.
3. a. The bit in a horse's mouth.
   b. The rudder of a ship.
4. They both guide and direct.
5. A small fire that can burn a great forest.
6. a. It is a fire.
   b. A world of wickedness.
   c. Contaminates and depraves the whole body.
   d. Stirs up evil.
7. Satan—it is set on fire by hell.
8. The fruit of your mouth.
9. Death and life.
10. a. Rash Speaking—pierces like thrusts of a sword.
    b. Wise Speaking—brings healing.
11. a. Gentle—turns away wrath.
    b. Wise—makes knowledge acceptable.
    c. Soothing—a tree of life.
12. a. Harsh—stirs up anger.
    b. Fools—spout folly.
    c. Perverse—crushes the spirit.
    d. Fools—bring strife.
    e. His mouth calls for blows.
    f. His mouth is his ruin—will snare his soul.
13. a. Filthiness.
    b. Silly talk.
    c. Coarse jesting.
14. A madman who throws firebands, arrows and death.
15. Contention.
16. a. Charcoal to hot embers.
    b. Wood to fire.
17. The innermost parts of the body.
18. Hatred.
19. a. His wickedness will be revealed before the assembly.
    b. He will dig a pit and fall into it.
    c. He will roll a stone and it will come back on him.
    d. Every careless word will be accounted for on the day of judgment.
    e. By your words you will be justified and by your words you shall be condemned.
20. That which fills the heart.
21. No.
22. Yes—through Jesus.
23. a. Confess your sins to one another and pray for one another that you may be healed.
    b. Love you enemies, pray for those who persecute you.
    c. Forgive your brother from your heart.
    d. Cleanse your mind with the Word.

24. a. Do not give the devil an opportunity.
    b. Let no unwholesome word proceed from your mouth.
    c. Speak only that which edifies.
    d. Speak only that which gives grace.
    e. Do not grieve the Holy Spirit.
    f. Let all bitterness, wrath, anger, clamor and slander be put away from you.
    g. Be kind to one another, tender-hearted.
    h. Forgive each other just as God has forgiven you.

STUDY 6

THE WORDS OF OUR MOUTH AND THE MEDITATIONS OF OUR HEART

Correct Answers

1. a. A restless evil.
   b. Full of deadly poison.
   c. Brings blessings.
   d. Brings cursings.
   e. Gives fresh and bitter water.
2. They are pure as silver refined seven times.
3. Treasure them in our hearts.
4. a. Receive God's Word.
   b. Be attentive to wisdom.
   c. Incline your heart to understanding.
   d. Cry for discernment.
   e. Lift your voice for understanding.
   f. Seek her as silver.
   g. Search for her as for hidden treasures.
5. a. Then you will discern the fear of the Lord.
   b. You will discern the knowledge of God.
   c. Wisdom will enter your heart.
   d. Knowledge will be pleasant to your soul.
   e. Discretion will guard you.
   f. Understanding will watch over you.
   g. You will be delivered from the way of evil and from speaking perverse things.
6. a. Restore the soul.
   b. Make wise the simple.
   c. Rejoice the heart.
   d. Enlighten the eyes.
   e. Warns.
7. a. Treasure hidden in a field.
   b. A pearl of great value.
8. Things hidden since the foundation of the world.
9. It is not revealed to everyone, but is revealed to those who are disciples only.
10. Jesus will, through the Holy Spirit.
11. The spiritual is not first, but the natural; then the spiritual. (Behind the natural is a spiritual meaning).
12. a. The world.
    b. The sons of the kingdom.
    c. The sons of the evil one.
    d. The Kingdom of our Father.
    e. The devil.
    f. The end of the age.
    g. The angels (messengers).
    h. Hell.
13. a. The church.
    b. Satan.
    c. Authority and guidance of Satan and the world system.
    d. Bondage of Satan.
    e. Power of the Spirit.
14. The yoke of Satan will be broken and God's glory will fill the whole earth.

15. a. 1. Satan and his angels and those men who have turned their back on God.
      2. The Lamb and His chosen ones will overcome the satanic powers.
    b. The glory of God will outshine the sun and the moon.
16. a. Satan.
    b. Word of God.
    c. The voice of the Lord (His word in the mouth of His saints).
    d. Word anointed by the Spirit.
    e. Where the Word has been tried.
    f. Those who trust in the Lord.
    Interpretation: The Lord will punish Satan with His Word. Satan will fall by the Word, and it will devour him. His princes will be terrified at the voice of the Lord going forth from the mouth of His saints. The Lord declares this, whose name anointed Word is in those who trust Him and whose Word has been tried in those who trust Him.
17. a. Church.
    b. Jesus.
    c. Complete light (Jesus is complete light).
    d. The completion of creation in God's image.
    Interpretation: The light of the Church will be as the light of Jesus (a body in His image and likeness) whose complete light, revelation of Himself, will shine forth bringing about the completion of the creation, bearing the image of God.
18. Music and praise.
19. We will be blessed, happy.
20. a. Better than silver or gold.
    b. More precious than jewels.
    c. Long life, riches and honor.
    d. Brings pleasantness and peace to you.
    e. A tree of life.
21. a. Apples of gold.
    b. An earring and ornament of gold.
    c. Like the cold of snow in the time of harvest, it will refresh the soul.

STUDY 7

GODLY WISDOM, WORLDLY FRIENDSHIP AND OUR ATTITUDE TOWARD SINNERS

Correct Answers

1. With gentleness.
2. a. Bitter jealousy.
   b. Selfish ambition.
   c. Earthly.
   d. Natural.
   e. Demonic.
3. Demonic.
4. a. Disorder.
   b. Every evil thing.
5. a. Pure.
   b. Peaceable.
   c. Gentle.
   d. Reasonable.
   e. Full of mercy.
   f. Full of good fruits.
   g. Unwavering.
   h. Without hypocrisy.
6. Righteousness.
7. Abraham. He put others before himself, he did not have selfish ambition.
8. a. People seeking their own pleasures.
   b. Lust and envy.
9. Murder. Hating your brother.
10. You do not have because you do not ask.
11. They ask with wrong motives.
12. Friendship with the world.
13. a. Loving the ways of the world and the things in it.
    b. Lust of the flesh.
    c. Lust of the eyes.
    d. Boastful pride of life.
14. a. It is hostility toward God.
    b. Enemy of God.
15. a. Receive sinners.
    b. Eat with sinners.
    c. Love sinners.
    d. Die to self for them.
16. A. The lost sheep.
    His attitude:
    a. Goes after him.
    b. Rejoices over finding him.
    c. Rejoices with his friends over him.
    d. Great joy in heaven over his repentance.
       1. On His shoulders.
       2. The government—His shoulders.
       3. The names of the sons of Israel.

16. B. The lost coin.
His attitude:
a. Searches carefully for him.
b. Lights a lamp and sweeps the house.
c. Rejoices over him.
d. Joy over his repentance.
   1. The believers.
C. The prodigal son.
a. Compassion.
b. Embraced him.
c. Ran to him and kissed him.
d. Bestows gifts upon him.
e. Celebration—the fatted calf.
f. Merry.
   1. Proud.
   2. Jealous.
   3. a. He had always been with the Father.
      b. All that was the Father's was his.
17. When man recognizes that it is God who rules.
18. a. He raised his eyes toward heaven.
b. His reason [knowledge] was returned to him.
c. He blessed the Most High and praised and honored Him who lives forever.
19. All the inhabitants of the earth are accounted as nothing.
20. a. His reason [knowledge] returned.
b. His majesty and splendor was restored.
c. His counselors and nobles began seeking him out.
d. He was established in sovereignty.
e. Surpassing greatness was added to him.
21. He praises, honors and exalts the Lord, recognizing the God is King. He acknowledges that he has been humbled by God.

STUDY 8

GOD'S LOVE, OUR HUMILITY, AND THE DEVIL'S PERSECUTION

Correct Answers

1. He jealously desires us.
2. That He would destroy the physical temple and raise it up in three days.
3. When Jesus' physical body was destroyed, His Spirit departed. At the very same this happened the Spirit of God left the Holy of Holies in the temple at Jerusalem.
4. In us.
5. a. If we forgive the sins of any, their sins have been forgiven them.
   b. The one who joins himself to the Lord is one spirit with Him.
6. The proud.
7. a. As brothers.
   b. The servant.
8. Humility.
9. a. Submit yourselves to God, resist the devil.
   b. Humble yourself under the hand of God, resist the devil.
10. Pride goes before destruction.
11. a. To hate evil.
    b. To hate pride.
    c. To hate arrogance.
    d. To hate the perverted mouth.
12. a. Be of sober spirit.
    b. Be on the alert.
    c. Gird your minds for action.
    d. Fix your hope completely on the grace to be brought to you at the revelation of Jesus.
13. a. In the mind.
    b. By destroying speculations.
    c. Destroy every lofty thing raised up against the knowledge of God.
    d. Taking every thought captive to the obedience of Christ.
14. He will flee.
15. Knowing that the same experiences of suffering are being accomplished by your brethren who are in the world.
16. By letting the sun go down on your anger.
17. a. Strengthen one another.
    b. Encourage one another to continue in the faith.
    c. Through many tribulations we must enter the kingdom of God.
18. a. Paul suffered affliction being imprisoned for Jesus' sake.
    b. John was exiled to Patmos, being a fellow partaker in tribulation.
    c. Jesus was hated and persecuted.
    d. We will have tribulation and persecution.
19. a. Do not revile in return.
    b. Utter no threats.
    c. Love your enemies and pray for them.
20. We will reign with Him.

THE DILIGENT SEEKER, THE REPENTANT HEART, THE RIGHTEOUS JUDGMENT

Correct Answers

1. He will draw near to us.
2. He will let you find Him.
3. a. We must believe that He is.
   b. That He is a rewarder of those who seek Him.
4. a. Keep on asking.
   b. Keep on seeking.
   c. Keep on knocking.
5. a. Everyone who keeps on asking, receives.
   b. He who keeps on seeking, finds.
   c. To him who keeps on knocking, it will be opened.
6. a. Full assurance of understanding.
   b. True knowledge of God.
   c. All the treasures of wisdom and knowledge.
7. His Word tells us He will.
8. a. Cleanse your hands.
   b. Purify your hearts.
9. Double-minded.
10. Evil.
11. a. Cease to do evil.
    b. Learn to do good.
    c. Seek justice.
    d. Reprove the ruthless.
    e. Defend the orphan.
    f. Plead for the widow.
12. a. Obedient will eat the best of the land.
    b. Disobedient will be devoured by the sword.
13. a. Miserable, mourn and weep.
    b. Laughter turned into mourning.
    c. Joy turned to gloom.
    d. Humbled before the Lord.
14. a. Do not speak against one another.
    b. Do not judge a brother.
    c. If you speak against the law, you condemn the law.
15. Love your neighbor as yourself.
16. One who spreads strife among brothers.
17. God.
18. Judge those within the church.
19. a. Not according to appearance.
    b. As He heard from God, He judged.
20. a. Jesus did nothing on His own initiative.
    b. As He heard, He judged.
    c. His judgment was just.
    d. He did not seek His own will, but God's.
    e. We can, when the Father is with us in it.
21. Man looks at the outward appearance, but the Lord looks at the heart.
22. a. Those who feared God.
    b. Those who hated dishonest gain.
    c. Men of truth.

THE DILIGENT SEEKER, THE REPENTANT HEART, THE RIGHTEOUS JUDGMENT

STUDY 10

OUR ATTITUDE TOWARD THE FUTURE

Correct Answers

1. If the Lord wills, we shall live and also do this or that.
2. We do not know what our life will be like tomorrow.
3. Every form of greed.
4. If man tries to supply his own needs through his own efforts, according to his own will, it will end in vain.
5. Do not be anxious for your life.
6. a. Ravens.
   b. Lilies.
   c. Grass.
7. a. Thinking that by being anxious you can cause yourself to grow in physical stature.
   b. If you cannot do this very little thing, why are you anxious about other matters?
8. We are more valuable than the birds, and God takes care of them, so He will take care of all our needs.
9. a. Do not seek what you shall eat.
   b. Do not seek what you shall drink.
   c. Do not keep worrving.
10. They are eagerly seeking after these things.
11. a. The Father knows that we need these things.
    b. Seek for His Kingdom.
    c. These things shall be added to you.
12. To give us the kingdom.
13. Wisdom, knowledge, and joy.
14. a. Gathering and collecting.
    b. That He may give it to one who is good in His sight.
15. a. Misery.
    b. Riches will vanish.

STUDY 11

LIVING IN THE LAST DAYS AND PATIENT ENDURANCE

Correct Answers

1. Until the precious produce of the soil receives the early and late rains.
2. The saints will be full of the Word. Their hearts will overflow with joy and they will be anointed with the Holy Spirit. Everything that has been stripped away from the church that made it desolate will be restored. The name of the Lord will be praised. There will be knowledge of who God is and complete acknowledgement of His Lordship. The saints will never be put to shame.
3. After this God will pour out His Spirit upon all flesh.
4. a. Be patient.
   b. Strengthen your hearts.
5. a. By your perseverance you will win your souls.
   b. The one who has endured to the end will be saved.
6. It is at hand.
7. Do not complain against one another that you may not be judged, for the Judge is at the door.
8. a. Love your neighbor.
   b. Awaken from sleep.
   c. Lay aside the deeds of darkness.
   d. Avoid carousing, drunkenness, sexual promiscuity, sensuality, strife and jealousy.
   e. Put on Jesus and make no provision for the flesh.
9. a. The end of all things is at hand.
   b. Be of sound judgment and sober spirit for the purpose of prayer.
   c. Keep fervent in your love for one another.
10. The prophets.
11. a. God promised them a land or country.
    b. They lived as aliens, dwelling in tents.
    c. They died in faith without receiving the promises, but saw them and welcomed them.
    d. They confessed their vision.
12. a. Stoned and sawn in two.
    b. Tempted and put to death by the sword.
    c. Wore sheepskins, destitute, afflicted, ill-treated.
    d. Wandered.
    e. Gained approval through their faith.
    f. They did not receive what was promised.
13. Those who endure.
14. a. Job.
    b. He restored Job's fortunes.
    c. He increased all that he had, two-fold.
    d. His family and friends returned to him bearing gifts.
    e. His latter days were more blessed than his beginning.
    f. He had 14,000 sheep, 6,000 camels, 1,000 yoke of oxen and 1,000 female donkeys.
    g. He had seven sons and three daughters, the fairest in the land.
    h. He lived after the testing, 140 years and saw four generations.
15. a. Lay aside every encumbrance and sin.
    b. Run with endurance the race set before us.
    c. Fix our eyes on Jesus.
16. a. Consider Jesus who endured such hostility by sinners against Himself.
    b. We have not yet resisted to the point of shedding blood in striving against sin.

STUDY 12

CONCLUSION

Correct Answers

1. Make no oaths, but let your yes be yes, and your no, no.
2. Jesus did not try to defend Himself. His Word was true.
3. a. Pray.
   b. Sing praises.
4. Call on Him in the day of trouble and He will rescue you.
5. Singing with thankfulness.
6. Call for the elders of the church and let them pray over him, anointing him with oil in the name of the Lord.
7. a. The prayer offered in faith will restore the one who is sick.
   b. The Lord will raise him up.
   c. If he has committed sins, they will be forgiven him.
8. Sin.
9. Confess your sins to one another.
10. Many of the believers in Ephesus kept coming, confessing and disclosing their practices.
11. a. To bring good news to the afflicted.
    b. To bind up the brokenhearted.
    c. To proclaim liberty to the captives.
    d. To preach freedom to prisoners.
    e. To comfort all who mourn.
    f. To give a garland and the oil of gladness.
    g. To teach people how to praise the Lord.
12. It can accomplish much. Elijah prayed that it would not rain, and it did not rain for three years and six months. Then he prayed again and it rained.
    Jesus.
13. Abraham interceded for Sodom.
14. a. One who is God-fearing.
    b. One who does His will.
15. God will hear our prayers.
16. a. Be anxious for nothing.
    b. Let your requests be made known to God.
17. The peace of God will guard your hearts and minds.
18. You will save his soul from death and cover a multitude of sins.
19. a. Go and reprove him in private.
    b. Take one or two more with you if he doesn't repent.
    c. If he still doesn't repent, tell it to the church.
    d. If he still doesn't repent, let him be to you as a Gentile and a tax-gatherer.
20. a. Restore them in spirit of gentleness.
    b. Looking to yourselves, lest you too be tempted.

Life Changing Books & Bible Studies
from Maranatha Publications

Bible Study Series

Firm Foundation

This study is our best seller. Covers the foundational truths in Scripture. Includes repentance, baptism, healing, faith, and other studies. Paperback, 125 pages, $11.95
ISBN # 0-938553-005

Overcoming Life

Takes you a step further than the basics. Includes a series on brokenness, as well as faith, righteousness, and the work of the ministry. Paperback, 113 pages, $11.95
ISBN # 0-938558-01-3

Lovers of God

Life Changing truths from Philippians. The all-sufficiency of God, living in joy, victory over trials, having the mind of Christ, and fruitfulness in ministry. Paperback, 43 pages, $9.95
ISBN # 0-938558-03-X

Preparation of the Bride

Explains metaphors and hidden truths in the Song of Solomon. This study reveals the beauty of the union between Jesus and His Bride. Paperback, 234 pages, $16.95
ISBN # 0-88270-471-0

Life of Excellence

Help for building character in your Christian life… bridling the tongue, godly wisdom, our attitude toward sinners, living in the last days, and more. Paperback, 60 pages, $9.95
ISBN # 0-938558-04-8

Estudios Biblicos para un Fundamento Firmé

Firm Foundation Also Available in Spanish!

An interactive Bible Study that challenges the reader to utilize their Bible and seek out truths in Scripture. This top selling Bible study is used around the world. Paperback, 125 pages, $11.95
ISBN # 0-938558-22-6

Christian Perspectives

Biblical Views on Important Issues

These books are inspiring resources for Christian educators and all who want to challenge themselves to think and act on subjects of intellectual and social concern.

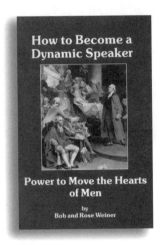

How to Become a Dynamic Speaker
by Bob & Rose Weiner

Christians are called to be the greatest communicators in the world. Do you desire to speak fearlessly with power to move the hearts of men? This book offers inspiring, practical advice that will help you become a more effective communicator.

paperback, 19 pages, $2.50
ISBN 0-938558-19-6

Mightier Than the Sword
by Bob & Rose Weiner
This book emphasizes the value of writing to develop the thinking and reasoning processes as well as offers practical suggestions to help you learn how to give written expression to your inner thoughts.

paperback, 20 pages, $2.50
ISBN 0-938558-16-1

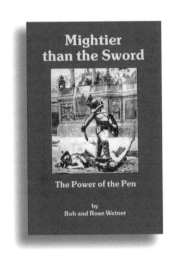

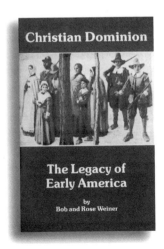

Christian Dominion: The Legacy of Early America
by Bob & Rose Weiner
This book presents the mandate for Christian dominion which enabled our founders to build a nation unlike any other in the history of the world.

paperback, 27 pages, $2.50
ISBN 0-938558-10-2

More Christian Perspectives

Biblical Views on Important Issues
These books are thought provoking treatments of various issues
including Christian economics and lieterature.

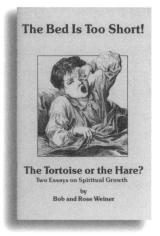

The Bed is Too Short
by Bob & Rose Weiner
The children's story of the tortoise and the hare has much
spiritual applicaiton. Practical advice on how to develop a
sensitivity to the still small voice of God and how to rise above
your circumstances and walk in God's grace.
paperback, 35 pages, $2.50
ISBN 0-938558-80-8

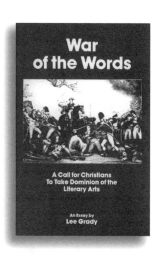

War of the Words
by Lee Grady
Humanists and atheists have affected society through
literature while Christians have had little influence in this field.
This book offers a challenge for Christians to take dominion of
the literary arts.
paperback, 18 pages, $2.50
ISBN 0-938558-11-0

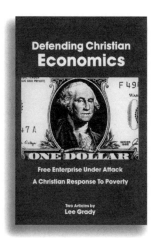

Defending Christian Economics
by Lee Grady
This book examines the Biblical system of economics —
individual enterprise — and looks at the Christian solution to
poverty. This message is an important weapon in the battle
against Marxist philosophy.
paperback, 26 pages, $2.50
ISBN 0-938558-12-9

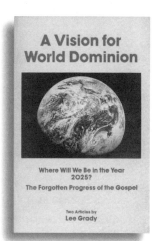

A Vision for World Dominion
by Lee Grady
The two articles in this book, "Where Will We Be in the Year
2025?" and "The Forgotten Progress of the Gospel" remind us
that Jesus Christ intends to rule planet earth and to pour out
His Spirit in world-wide revival.
paperback, 21 pages, $2.50
ISBN 0-938558-13-7

Life Changing Historical Reprints

from Maranatha Publications

The Story of Liberty

originally published in 1879.

The secular humanists have edited God out of history! Now you can read what they cut out. Reprinted from the original 1879 edition, *The Story of Liberty* tells you the price that was paid for our freedom and how it was won. An excellent historical resource for your library. This is our best seller among home schools and Christian educators. Paperback, illustrated, 415 pages, $14.95 ISBN 0-938558-20-X

The Story of Liberty Study Guide – Written by Steve Dawson, this workbook offers 98 pages of challenging comprehensive questions that allow the reader to fill-in-the-blank as they progress through this valuable study book. $10.95 ISBN 0-938558-27-7

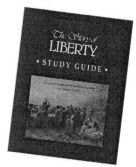

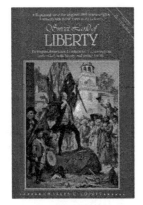

Sweet Land of Liberty

originally published in 1881 and titled *Old Times in the Colonies*

Sweet Land of Liberty is the sequel to *The Story of Liberty*. It tells the historical highlights of colonial America from a Providential view. This volume covers the period from the discovery and settlement of America to the Revolutionary War. Written by Civil War correspondent and children's author Charles Coffin, *Sweet Land of Liberty* has been faithfully reproduced exactly as it was originally printed in 1881. Paperback, illustrated, 458 pages, $14.95 ISBN 0-938558-48-X

The Boys of '76

reprinted from the original 1876 manuscript

In this powerful volume an attempt has been made to give a concise, plain, and authentic narrative of the principal battles of the Revolution as witnessed by those who took part in them. More than a century has passed since "*The Boys of '76*" shouldered their muskets and fought for their liberties. Author Charles Coffin brings to life the battles of the Revolution from "The Alarm" proclaimed in Concord in 1775, to the surrender of the British army in 1981. Paperback, illustrated, 423 pages, $16.95. ISBN 0-938558-82-X

"An accurate story of our nation's fight for liberty. I pray everyone, young and old alike, will read and remember *The Boys of '76.*"

Greg Harris, Director of Noble Institute and author of *The Christian Home School*

MARANATHA PUBLICATIONS, INC.

P. O. BOX 1799 • GAINESVILLE, FL 32602 • 352-375-6000 • FAX 352-335-0080

Bible Study Books— *by Bob and Rose Weiner*

BOOK NAME	PRICE	QUANTITY	TOTAL
Firm Foundation	$ 11.95		
Overcoming Life	$ 11.95		
Lovers of God	$ 9.95		
Life of Excellence	$ 9.95		
Preparation of the Bride	$16.95		
One Set of Above Studies (5)	$55.75		
Jesus Brings New Life	$ 5.95		
Spanish Firm Foundation	$ 11.95		

Christian History Books

BOOK NAME	PRICE	QUANTITY	TOTAL
The Story of Liberty (A Christian History Text)	$14.95		
Story of Liberty Study Guide - by Steve Dawson	$ 10.95		
Sweet Land of Liberty (Sequel to Story of Liberty)	$14.95		
The Boys of '76 (Sequel to Sweet Land of Liberty)	$16.95		

Booklets

BOOK NAME	PRICE	QUANTITY	TOTAL
— by Bob and Rose Weiner			
How to Become a Dynamic Speaker	$ 2.50		
Mightier Than The Sword	$ 2.50		
The Bed Is Too Short	$ 2.50		
Christian Dominion	$ 2.50		
— by Lee Grady			
Defending Christian Economics	$ 2.50		
A Vision For World Dominion	$ 2.50		
War of the Words	$ 2.50		

Sub Total	
Shipping	
Add FL sales tax	
TOTAL US Dollars	

VISA and MasterCard Accepted

Ship To:

Name _____

Address _____

City _____

State _____ Zip _____

Phone (_____) _____

❑ Check enclosed, payable to Maranatha Publications, Inc.

❑ Charge to my: ❑ VISA ❑ MasterCard

Card No. _____ Expires ____/____

Shipping & Handling:

Less than $10.00	$3.50
$10.00 - $24.99	$4.50
$25.00 - $49.99	$5.50
$50.00 or more	9%

Mail Order To: **Maranatha Publications, Inc., P.O. Box 1799, Gainesville, FL 32602**
Visit our websie at www.mpi2000.net